Know About Jawaharlal Nehru

MAPLE KIDS

KNOW ABOUT JAWAHARLAL NEHRU

ALL RIGHTS RESERVED. No part of this book may be reproduced in a retrieval system or transmitted in any form or by any means electronics, mechanical, photocopying, recording and or without permission of the publisher.

Published by

MAPLE PRESS PRIVATE LIMITED
office: A-63, Sector 58, Noida 201301, U.P., India
phone: +91 120 455 3581, 455 3583
email: info@maplepress.co.in
website: www.maplepress.co.in

Reprinted in 2019

ISBN: 978-93-50333-34-1

Contents

Preface 5
1. The Developing Years 6
2. Education 10
3. Jawaharlal Returns to India 14
4. Indira Priyadarshini 17
5. Freedom Struggle 21
6. Swaraj 24
7. Simon Commission 27
8. The Salt Satyagraha 30
9. Autobiography of Nehru 33
10. The Discovery of India 36
11. The Second World War 39
12. The Quit India Movement 41
13. Partition 44
14. The Constituent Assembly 46
15. Nehru Becomes Prime Minister 49
16. Issue of Pakistan 52
17. Kashmir 55
18. The Policy of Non-Alignment 58
19. Supporter of Peace 61
20. India-China Relationship 64
21. Differences over the Border 68
22. Nehru-The Great Follower of Democracy 72
23. The Man of Strength 75
24. End of the Great Soul 78

Preface

Jawaharlal Nehru (November 14, 1889 – May 27, 1964) was a leader of the moderate socialist wing of the Indian National Congress during and after India's struggle for independence from the British Empire. He became the first Prime Minister of India at independence on August 15, 1947; holding the office until his death.

He is the son of the Congress leader Motilal Nehru. He pursued his education in England and practiced law before following his father into politics. He was a follower of Mahatma Gandhi and was the President of Congress for the first time in 1929.

As the Prime Minister, Nehru took up a foreign policy of non-alignment while pursuing India's claim to Kashmir with Pakistan in the opposition. This resulted in the First Kashmir War (1947-49).

His only daughter, Indira, went on to become Prime Minister after the death of his successor, Lal Bahadur Shastri, in January 1966.

This book sums up the life history of Jawaharlal Nehru and gives an account of his freedom struggle.

CHAPTER 1
The Developing Years

India's first Prime Minister, Jawaharlal Nehru was born on 14 November 1889 in Allahabad. A Kashmiri Brahmin by religion, he lived in the Civil Lines which was mostly dwelled by Europeans. His father, Motilal Nehru was a rich and reputed lawyer by profession and his mother, Swarup Rani, was charming and a holy woman. The couple had three children, Jawaharlal being the only brother among his two sisters, Swarup and Krishna.

He was removed within a short duration of six months from St. Mary's Convent School where he was given initial admittance. So, he was primarily homeschooled. During the course of which, he met with Ferdinand Brooks. He was a young man in his early twenties, who was his English tutor for his home study. He was also one of the factors that were responsible for his interest in literature. Under his guidance, Jawaharlal read several books on religion and science. But he never forgot his love for English Literature.

His interests in religion made him come across an Irish woman, Mrs. Annie Besant, who inspired him a

lot. He decided to join the *Theosophical Society* that was founded by her. The society focused on religious thoughts and wanted to familiarize the world with the history of India. But, he couldn't commit for long, as he believed in action just like his father.

Except for his academic explorations, he also participated in several extra-curricular activities like swimming, tennis and cricket. Jawaharlal Nehru was also influenced and affected by the Mughals and the British. He was against the British rule, but was totally fluent in

English language. Later, at the age of fourteen, a war broke out between Japan and Russia. He was deeply affected by it as he had always thought of Asian and Indian freedom in the same angle.

In 1905, Motilal Nehru shifted with his family to England. At the age of fifteen, Jawaharlal was admitted to a famous Public School at Harrow. As he had never stayed without his parents before, he grew homesick. Even the company of his other British friends failed to give him much comfort. His interests in sports and studies started dwindling. In academics, he found himself to be good at general knowledge, but weak in Latin.

CHAPTER 2
Education

The Wright Brothers, who made their first flight in the air, inspired him a lot. Jawaharlal was excited at the possibility of touching the sky. This incident inspired him to concentrate on his studies. Soon, he started excelling in academics. He also participated in various co-curricular activities like the Rifle Club and the Cadet corps at school.

The feeling of isolation seeped in when he came to know about the Swadeshi movement in India. This movement preached complete rejection and non-use of British goods. He felt disconnected as he was unable to talk or discuss about this with anyone in Harrow. But finally, in the summer of 1906, he visited his parents for three weeks in Mussoorie. Back in England, he wrote his comments on Indian politics to his father and asked for more information in return.

In the next few years, Jawaharlal felt an urgency to join the university by completing his education at Harrow. In October 1907, Jawaharlal joined the Trinity College,

Cambridge, when he was just approaching eighteen. Though his subjects were limited to Chemistry, Geology and Botany, his interests were much wider. During his stay in Cambridge, and even during his holidays in London, he met with several people. He interacted, and discussed with them various topics on literature, history, books, politics, and economics.

He found these subjects difficult at first, but as soon as he started reading, he found them interesting. He came across various socialist ideas and was greatly influenced by the ideas of Bernard Shaw and Bertrand Russell.

He lived his life on his own terms. He had an all-round experience of life, including work, games, and enjoyment. By this time, he had decided to join the Indian freedom struggle. When his father joined the struggle, he tried to gather and update himself with the events that were happening back in India. But his ways of action were

serious as compared to the milder ways of his father's politics.

In 1909, Jawaharlal Nehru graduated from The Trinity College with a second class degree in Natural Science. After graduating, he planned to join the Indian Civil Services. But had to drop the idea primarily for two reasons. Firstly, he was too young to appear for the examination. Secondly, his father feared that once he gets selected, he would be posted in some remote place and would be separated from his parents yet again.

Therefore, he decided to join the bar, just like his father. He successfully cleared the bar. He returned to India in 1912, after spending a period of seven years in England.

CHAPTER 3
Jawaharlal Returns to India

When Jawaharlal returned to India, Indian politics didn't seem to interest him. The Nationalist groups were divided into two categories namely the extremists and the moderates. The extremists were those who strongly reacted against the British. The moderates were those who believed in balancing, planning and working. At that time, the group was without a leader as Tilak, the leader of the extremists, was in prison.

On the other hand, the moderates, along with the Congress, were helping the British. The Congress was an extension of the moderates.

In 1921, on the occasion of Christmas, Jawaharlal was sent as a member to the Congress session at Bankipore. He was highly disappointed seeing everyone expensively dressed for the session. This made the session look more of a social gathering than a political meeting. In addition to that, the attendees were busy conversing in English which made the whole gathering look like a high class event thus, failing the core purpose of the session.

He joined the High Court; but the dull, boring routine killed his interest. Though he visited the bar library and the club regularly, he still got bored of meeting the same old people every time. Therefore, he started searching for other means of enjoyment like hunting and outings. He leaned towards politics, but there was no scope of politics at that time. Nevertheless, he joined the Congress, as for him politics was to revolt against the foreign rule. He worked for the party at times of action.

The First World War broke out in 1914. The British Government forced India to participate in the war. Though India had a neutral attitude, Jawaharlal had a slight liking towards the French, who were fighting for the British.

After the war was over, India continued its revolt against the British rule. Tilak was released from the prison. He immediately started an organization with Mrs. Besant. Their motive was to demand freedom from the

British rule. This came to be known as The Home Rule League. Many speeches and the displays were conducted by The Home Rule League which gained a lot of attention. Resulting in the arrest of the founding member of the League, Mrs. Annie Besant. This further agitated the moderates.

CHAPTER 4
Indira Priyadarshini

Jawaharlal became an active member of the party and started participating in all its proceedings. He made his first appearance in 1915, by making a formal speech to the public at Allahabad. The meeting was held to protest against the new law. As he had spent his early years in abroad, he felt shy and uncomfortable in delivering the speech in Hindi. But nevertheless, he refused to speak to the public in English. In spite of this, he impressed the public as well as the leaders who attended the meeting and was applauded for his speech.

The year 1916 holds much significance. Firstly, during a session of the Lucknow Congress, Jawaharlal first met with Gandhi. Gandhi was already quite influential by that time. Soon Motilal and Jawaharlal became well acquainted with him and started to closely engage and work with him. Secondly, in 1916 Nehru married Kamala Kaul, a brave, pretty, and holy woman. She carried out her wifely duties and supported Jawaharlal throughout his life. Even in her last days, she stood by his side like a pillar of strength.

Indira Priyadarshini, the daughter of Jawaharlal and Kamala Nehru, was born on 19th November 1917. She later became the first woman Prime Minister of India.

Just a year later, in 1918, the uneventful Jallianwala Bagh massacre occurred in which hundreds and thousands of people were killed. Jawaharlal, along with Gandhi, arrived at the spot of mass murder. They were shocked to see such cruelty done to the people. Later Gandhi expressed his extreme disgust and wrote a report on the tragic massacre. His report was later presented at the Congress meeting. On the other hand, the British also held an inquiry. The committee issued severe punishment against General Dyer, the man responsible for the whole tragic event.

By this time, Jawaharlal and Gandhi were well acquainted and shared a close connection with each

other. In 1919, Gandhi first proposed his program of non-violence in a Congress session held in Amritsar. Jawaharlal who already had a bitter spot for the British, fought with the officials. Due to sudden ill-health of his wife and his mother, Jawaharlal had to take them to Mussoorie. At that time, an Afghan representative was scheduled to come to India to hold peace talks with the Government. The Afghans, like the Indians, were also fighting against the British. So, in order to stop Jawaharlal from meeting the Afghan representative, the government ordered him to leave the district within twenty-four hours. Unwillingly, Jawaharlal returned to Allahabad.

CHAPTER 5
Freedom Struggle

At this time, Jawaharlal happened to meet the farmers of the United Provinces. Over two thousand farmers were camping on the banks of Yamuna. They requested him to listen to their plea and sufferings. They informed him about the dominance of landlords of the United Provinces who extracted money from the poor farmers in order to pay off their taxes to the government. This affected the

economy of the farmers. In case they fail to pay, they were immediately driven off the land. In such a condition, they were completely blank and had nowhere else to go. He was moved after hearing their side of the story. When asked for help, Jawaharlal motivated them to help themselves. He asked them to muster courage and rise against the landlords. He kept advising and often spoke to them. He eventually lost his shyness in public speaking. Nehru helped them to know and approach their own issues and the villagers helped him to intimately know the village areas. This resulted in large participation of the farmers in the national movement under his leadership.

The non-cooperation movement had a popular head start. It attracted a lot of youth patriots its way who were ready to go to jail for the love of the nation. As a symbol for non-cooperation, they gave up everything that was foreign- be it schools, colleges or clothes. Many went to prison, along with Jawaharlal, when they didn't cooperate to welcome the Prince of Wales, in 1921.

The movement went on smoothly until in Chauri Chaura, a village in Uttar Pradesh, a crowd of farmers took up a violent step. They set fire to a police station and burnt half a dozen of policemen to death. Gandhi was deeply saddened by this incident. He immediately terminated the non-cooperation movement. This dissatisfied many leaders including Jawaharlal, who were in prison. After his release, Jawaharlal visited Gandhi in Ahmedabad in order to discuss his succeeding plans. But before he could reach, Gandhi was arrested. He was present when Gandhi was sentenced. When asked, Gandhi duly answered his charges. Everyone, including the British judge, was moved hearing his statements.

Jawaharlal was arrested when he returned to Allahabad for driving out shops selling foreign clothes. He was sentenced for eighteen months' of imprisonment. This created a doubt in the amount of freedom he carries. No one knew when and for how long he would be set free.

CHAPTER 6
Swaraj

With the imprisonment of Jawaharlal, came a pause in the non-cooperation movement. Many leaders were released. His passion and hard work forced him to keep himself busy. He was appointed as the General Secretary of the Congress and held that post from time to time.

In the meantime, the British introduced fresh reforms. New councils of ministers were formed. Most of the Congressmen including Jawaharlal Nehru refused to be appointed as ministers. But there were some Congressmen

who thought that they should be in the councils in order to truly fight against the ruling power. These Congressmen called themselves 'Swarajists' as they wanted 'Swaraj' or self-rule. And the Congressmen who refused to join the councils thinking it to be a waste of time were called the 'no-changers', i.e., those who would not change. They were loyal supporters of Gandhi and Jawaharlal was one of them.

This clash in attitudes created a division within the party members. The party members started finding fault in one another. The only thing they shared was their deep-seated respect for Gandhi. Unlike other Congressmen, Gandhi was not opposed to Swarajists. The Swarajists delivered speeches and even tried to propose their idea to the British government. But their demands remained unfulfilled.

In 1926, Kamala was hospitalized for tuberculosis. Later Jawaharlal along with Kamala and Indira went to Switzerland for her treatment. He was happy to take a break from the problems in India for some time. He needed to think and view the issue from a distance. He enjoyed his stay in Europe. He met several Indians who had left India and were living in Europe, who contributed to India's struggle in their own way.

In February 1927, the Congress of Oppressed Nationalities met in Brussels. Many prominent leaders of the colonized countries were present. At the meet,

Jawaharlal met the widow of Sun Yat Sen, who was a great leader of China. He also met Dr. Ho Chi-Minh, the leader of the Vietnamese people who were struggling against the French rule. Dr. Ho Chi-Minh was about to become the President of North Vietnam. Jawaharlal met with a lot of personalities. He noticed that their way of fighting for freedom was quite similar to his idea of struggle. He also realized that struggle against the colonial rule was a worldwide phenomenon.

CHAPTER 7
Simon Commission

Jawaharlal also went to the Soviet Union. The Russian revolt of 1917 introduced a new approach to Jawaharlal. He wanted India to follow its footsteps and tried his best to develop friendship between the two countries.

Jawaharlal came back from his trip to Europe. He had gathered many ideas and approaches that could be used to fight for India's freedom. At the Madras Congress session, in 1927, he presented his idea of complete independence from the British. This idea was against the impression of India as a British Kingdom, as viewed by other Congressmen. Gandhi did not support his idea and termed it impractical.

On the other hand, the British appointed the Simon Commission. This commission was headed by a reputed lawyer Simon as its chairman. Its motive was to judge whether India was ready for self-rule or 'Swaraj'. The absence of any Indian in its proceedings aroused doubt in the mind of the people. So they decided to avoid it and

protested against the commission by shouting 'Simon, go back!'

While protesting against the Simon Commission in Lucknow, Jawaharlal was attacked by the police and was hurt. He wanted to counterattack but was reminded of Gandhi's principles of non-violence. This incident triggered rage all over the country.

The clash in beliefs among Indians was clearly visible. The British wanted the Indians to agree on their project for self-rule. A conference of all parties was held under the chairmanship of Motilal Nehru. Neither the British accepted the project that was prepared by the conference nor did the Indians agree to the project prepared by the Simon Commission.

On December 1928, the Congress organized a meet in Calcutta. They wanted to resolve the differences in ideologies between the older and the younger generations. The former was led by Motilal Nehru and Gandhi. Jawaharlal Nehru and Subhas Chandra Bose represented the younger generation. The latter believed in immediate independence. The older leaders believed that India was not in a position to impose such a demand. They wanted to slowly approach the process slowly. Finally, they were able to sort out a compromise. They decided that the British have to grant India's independence within a year's notice, or else the Congress will fight for immediate independence.

CHAPTER 8
The Salt Satyagraha

At midnight, on 31st December 1929, the Congress declared independence by taking up a promise to fight for 'Poorna Swaraj'. On this day, Jawaharlal addressed the people that "I am a Socialist and a Republican". He wanted the people to know that his interest lies in theirs. He wanted Swaraj for the poor, not for the rich. He encouraged people to muster courage and take action.

When the British made no response to the Congress' proposal, the latter took up the promise for independence. As salt is the basic requirement for the living, Gandhi proposed to remove any taxations on salt. He also warned for a nationwide revolt, if rejected by the British. So, when the Viceroy rejected the proposals, Gandhi started preparing the country for the Satyagraha movement. He asked the people to start making salt illegally so that the salt law will be broken. The protest was led by Gandhi. He thought it to be the best way to revolt against the British rule.

On March 12, 1930, Gandhi marched along with other 'Satyagrahis' from his ashram at Sabarmati towards Dandi. He was accompanied by a large number of people. The group also included women who were affected by it and had started making salt. During the movement, many sacrificed their lives and many got arrested. Jawaharlal was also arrested and sentenced in Allahabad. Mahatma Gandhi was arrested when he reached Dandi. Even Motilal Nehru was arrested and was jailed in the same prison as his son, at Naini.

The Satyagraha movement was rising in success. The British had started to fear it, so they agreed to talk to the Congress leaders. Jawaharlal and Motilal were released from the jail. Suddenly Motilal fell ill. His death on 6th February 1931 created a vacuum in the lives of Gandhi and Jawaharlal Nehru. Gandhi felt as if he lost his closest friend, and Jawaharlal was grief-stricken.

Several sessions of talks were organized between the British Government and the moderate Indian leaders in London. These talks were named as Round Table Conferences. The first conference took place without the participation of the Congress leaders as they had refused to take part in it. But after an agreement with the Viceroy, Gandhi agreed to attend the second conference. This conference came to be known as the Gandhi-Irwin Agreement. It is sometimes referred as 'cease-fire' as this meet indicated a possibility of another struggle between the British and the Congress. But on the contrary, the Viceroy agreed to all of Gandhi's conditions.

8 Round Table Conference

CHAPTER 9
Autobiography of Nehru

The Congress met in Karachi and decided to send Gandhi as their representative to London. Gandhi arrived at the conference wearing a 'Dhoti' and shocked everyone through his speeches. As the British had no intention to grant Swaraj, the second Round Table Conference was also a failure. This highly disappointed Gandhi.

In India, the Gandhi-Irwin Agreement was broken. Both the British and the moderates started blaming Jawaharlal for the breakage. But in reality, it was the British officials who were responsible for the breaking of the agreement as they didn't want the agreement to succeed in the first place.

In the meanwhile, the farmers in the United Provinces under the leadership of Jawaharlal Nehru entered into a revolt against the British. This led to the arrest of Jawaharlal. Gandhi was informed of the arrest while he was returning from London. He himself got arrested soon after landing on the Indian soil. The Third Round Table Conference was organized without the Congress.

Jawaharlal was a man of action. He had repeated clashes with the government. He was often arrested and had to spend many years in prison. He has also been transferred to many jails- at Naini, Bareilly, Dehradun, Almora, Alipore in Calcutta, and Ahmadnagar. He still fought for independence. He tolerated the difficult life in prison cells, struggling with loneliness, and staying away from his family. Though he was allowed to receive books and journals in jail, the atmosphere in prison was still unbearable. But his courage, perseverance and determination saved him from losing his spirits. As he was a disciplinarian, he often engaged in mental and physical exercises to keep himself fit. His loneliness escapes for a while when he receives letters from his family and friends every fourteen days. Though he was lonely most of the times, he befriended many in prison. He discussed with them on most matters. His favourite pastime was gardening and reading books.

From 1931 to 1933, he frequently wrote letters to his little daughter, Indira. These letters were later published in the form of a book called the *Glimpses of World History*. From June 1934 to February 1935 he wrote his autobiography. It was later published in 1936. The book was published in England and eventually became famous. Jawaharlal also wrote a book during the most difficult days of his life. Struggling with the conflicts arising in his mind, he vented out his feelings and opinions without a censure. He freely criticized Gandhi and others in this book. He tried finding answers to the innumerable questions he had in his mind. This book gives an honest account of his life.

CHAPTER 10
The Discovery of India

Jawaharlal Nehru was imprisoned for nearly three years in Ahmadnagar Fort in 1941. During his time of imprisonment, he engaged himself in writing a book named *The Discovery of India*. The book highlights his attempt to discover India, its people, its culture, his love for his country and its people. Making the best use of the available time, he wrote three books while he was in prison.

The year 1932 was marked with severe domination which made people feel angry and helpless. On 17 August 1932, a separate electoral was granted to the untouchables. Mahatma Gandhi revolted against such a system and the electoral was removed by the British Government. It was finally decided that instead of being treated as an outcast, the untouchables would be considered as a part of the Hindu community. They were named 'Harijans' by Gandhi which meant the 'people of God'.

As Jawaharlal's mother became seriously ill in August 1933, he was released from jail. As soon as his mother's health showed some improvement, he met with Gandhi and other leaders. He started attending party meetings. He was about to get arrested, but was relieved as he had to go to Calcutta to consult a doctor for the ill health of his wife, Kamala.

On 15 January 1934, an earthquake resulted in large-scale destruction in Bihar. He immediately visited the place and condemned the government for not organizing necessary relief. When he returned back to Allahabad, he was arrested and sent to the Presidency Prison in Calcutta. Later that year, he was transferred to a prison in Dehradun. It was in Dehradun when he started writing his biography.

Towards the end of July, Kamala's condition grew worse and became critical. Due to her dwindling health, Jawaharlal was asked to go to Allahabad. He was again arrested on 25th August and sent to Naini Prison. Some weeks later, he was transferred to the district prison at Almora, so that he could be nearer to Kamala, who was at Bhowali for her treatment.

In September 1935, he was discharged from Almora Prison to accompany his wife to Germany in the month of May that year. In the meanwhile, Hitler was growing as a powerful leader in Germany and Mussolini in Italy. Coincidentally highlighting two of the greatest leaders of the time!

CHAPTER 11
The Second World War

Even after numerous attempts from his side, Jawaharlal lost his wife Kamala in 1936 and returned to India. After returning, he presided over the Lucknow session. The practice of colonial ruling was increasing especially in Britain, Italy, Germany and China. He presented this picture of the world to the Congress representative in Lucknow. They began to understand the universal connection that if there was no peace in the world then there could be no peace here.

As the President of the Congress, he continued to preach and spread his ideas. He gained the liking of the peasants and labourers. The youth respected him and he became their inspiration. Among the Congress leaders, he was very close to Gandhi. Due to his popularity among the masses, he was asked to lead the Congress for one more year. So, he presided over the Congress session at Faizpur.

The Second World War broke out in Europe, in September 1939. This served as an excuse for the British government to halt the independence of India till war ends. Jawaharlal wanted India to fight against Hitler, but unfortunately only a free country could have done so.

By 1937, the Congress had formed ministries in some provinces. Gandhi asked the people not to cooperate with the British in the war effort. To make the protest effective, he started a No-War Satyagraha movement in July 1940. Before Jawaharlal Nehru could offer Satyagraha, he was arrested for some speeches he had previously delivered in Gorakhpur. He was immediately tried and sentenced to four years imprisonment. The country was shocked at the severity of the sentence. Such a sentence was condemned, even in England. Gandhi was arrested in October 1940, but the Satyagraha went on.

Thousands of Congress workers were imprisoned. It was clear that the people had nothing to do with the war. The British felt that defending India without the cooperation of the Indian people was nearly impossible. It was followed by the release of the Congress leaders.

The British sent proposals to India through a senior minister, Sir Stafford Cripps. They were called the Cripps Proposals. It proposed partial deliverance of power to the Indians. This was ultimately rejected by Gandhi as he demanded complete freedom. But the British Government and Cripps did not agree and proposed that Indians would have other powers except their control over the defence side.

CHAPTER 12
The Quit India Movement

Two of the most important figures in Indian politics, i.e., Jawaharlal Nehru and Mahatma Gandhi greatly differed in their ideologies. On one hand, Gandhi was in favour of non-violence, whereas on the other, Jawaharlal was prompt in quick actions. There was a constant fear of Japanese taking over India anytime soon. Such a situation demanded immediate defensive action in order to protect the country. Jawaharlal Nehru accepted the fact and it

was agreed unanimously that immediate freedom was the only need of the time.

Despite of such differences in their ideologies, Jawaharlal and Gandhi rejected the ongoing rumour of internal clashes between them. They affirmed that they are not divided, but united. To this, Gandhi also added that Jawaharlal would definitely succeed him.

On the political platform, the situation was getting out of control. The colonial rule was ending all over the world but there was still no hope for India's independence from the British rule. The British stated that they can hand over the power only after the war ends and proposed a project that would divide India into two halves.

The Muslim League which is a Muslim organization, with Jinnah as its leader, demanded a separate nation for the Muslim community. This was later called the two-nation theory. Therefore, the British proposed to divide the country into India and Pakistan. This was outrightly rejected by the Congress including Gandhi. According to them, two different religions did not necessarily mean two separate countries. They wanted India to revive her lost glory and freedom in its entirety. But the British applied the propaganda of 'divide-and-rule'. They encouraged the Muslim League to demand for a division and carve out a separate nation solely for Muslims.

On 8 August, 1942, in the Bombay session, the Congress successfully passed the Quit India proposal.

On the occasion, Nehru and Gandhi delivered inspiring speeches. But their arrest on the very next day added an abrupt pause.

In February 1943, there was an increase in the intensity of revolt against the British government. As a reaction against the government, Gandhi fasted unto death. A year later, in May 1944, he held a meeting with Jinnah to discuss and seek an agreement between the Congress and the Muslim League. But unfortunately, the meeting failed.

The Second World War ended in the year 1945. A few months later, in July, the Labour Party came to power in Britain. It was evident that British would not be able to hold India for long after the war ended. Therefore, the Congress party wanted to take another attempt to settle India's demand for freedom. The great famine in 1943 led to the death of thousands of people which further aggravated the agitation and frustration among the masses.

CHAPTER 13
Partition

After the war ended, the new Viceroy of India, Lord Wavell tried to propose the same political settlement of dividing India into two countries. He organized various talks in Shimla with representatives from leading parties, but in vain. According to Jinnah, Muslim League was the only party that represented the Muslims. But the congress also argued to have favoured and represented Muslims. The English government was slowly losing control over its colonies, and new powers like America and Russia were emerging. Jawaharlal was excited at the idea of British imperialism coming to an end. The main issue that they were facing was from the Muslim League who wanted to carve a separate nation. Their demands were supported by the British government. The idea of dividing the country on the basis of religion did not make any sense to Jawaharlal and many others. According to Jawaharlal, India must not be restrictive in any sense. If any part of the country did not want to join the India Union, then it would not be forced to do so. He firmly believed that there should never be a partition on the basis of religion.

On February 1946, the British government formulated a Cabinet Mission consisting of three cabinet ministers, Lord Pethick- Lawrence, A. V. Alexander, and Sir Stafford Cripps. They coincidentally shared a close bonded friendship with Jawaharlal Nehru. After discussing with all the chief Indian leaders, they came up with two sets of proposals, the long-term and the short-term. The long-term proposal was in line with what Jawaharlal had proposed a long time ago of forming a Constitution making body or the Constituent Assembly. Jawaharlal had termed it as self-willpower which granted everyone the right to decide for his/her future. The long-term proposal permitted the non-participation of the existing states in the Indian Union if they don't want to. They had the freedom to remain as they are with no forced compulsion to join the Indian Union. The Congress, in order to avoid the partition, accepted the long-term proposal, while the British government encouraged for a partition. The short-term plan was for a temporary national government till a proper constitution was formed.

CHAPTER 14

The Constituent Assembly

The short-term plan consisted the representatives of the Congress, the Muslim League, and others. The Muslim League did not accept the short-term plan due to Jawaharlal insistence on the Congress's role to lead the Constituent assembly and shape India's freedom as it deemed right. It was believed that the acceptance of the short term proposal marked the non-participation of the Muslims in the formation of the Constitution.

On the contrary, Jawaharlal Nehru, the President of the Congress Committee, accepted the short-term proposal. His acceptance held significance as he was appointed in the Viceroy's Executive Council. The Cabinet was to work under the Vice-President, and therefore was almost equal to the Prime Minister. Various representatives of the Congress and of other parties were invited to form the government. Jawaharlal Nehru worked like the Prime Minister and was very active in his work. Sardar Patel, Dr. Rajendra Prasad, and Maulana Azad worked as members of the government.

The growing success of India and the failure of their 'divide-and-rule' propaganda left the British quite unhappy. This led them to pressurize the Muslim League to join the government. Some members were dropped from the Executive Council and members from the Muslim Council joined in their place. But instead of cooperating, their joint participation arose various internal conflicts and disturbances. The only motive of the Muslim league was to form a separate country for the Muslims.

The Constituent Assembly met in November. Jawaharlal, along with the members of the Muslim League tried their best to shape the freedom that India received.

Despite of such committees, the British had already planned things in their own way. It was decided by the British government to hand over the power to the people before June 1948. The Viceroy of India, Lord Mountbatten held meetings with various Indian leaders and 'June 3'

plan was prepared. It consisted of a totally new set of plan of action which proposed the division of India into two countries in 15 August 1947. Both the groups accepted it. But even after the division, the Muslim League failed to get what it wanted as the principal Hindu parts of Bengal, Punjab and Assam came on the part of India.

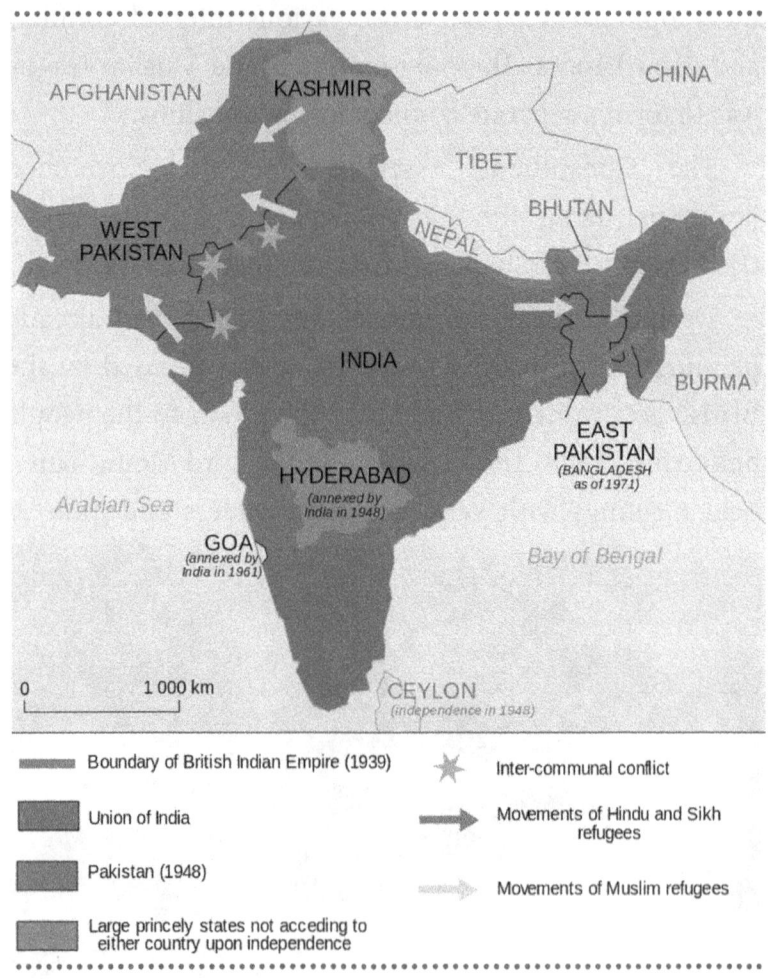

CHAPTER 15
Nehru Becomes Prime Minister

On 15 August 1947, at the age of fifty-eight, Jawaharlal Nehru took oath as the first Prime Minister of independent India. Though the country got its freedom, there were clouds of darkness all over the nation due to ongoing conflicts in Punjab where thousands of people were getting killed and uprooted. There were constant tensions in the North. There were continuous riots between the Hindus and the Muslims all over the country.

On 30 January 1948, Gandhi was shot dead by a Hindu named Nathuram Godse. The entire nation was in grief and pain. Jawaharlal Nehru felt as if he didn't only lose a co-worker, but also a friend, philosopher, and guide.

The sudden death of the Father of the Nation left Jawaharlal Nehru all alone in managing the whole nation. The burden of managing the entire country fell unto his shoulders. He was determined to tackle it with his hard work and perseverance. After the partition, the Muslim leaders felt as if they were in a minority. There were around fifty million Muslims in India and there were

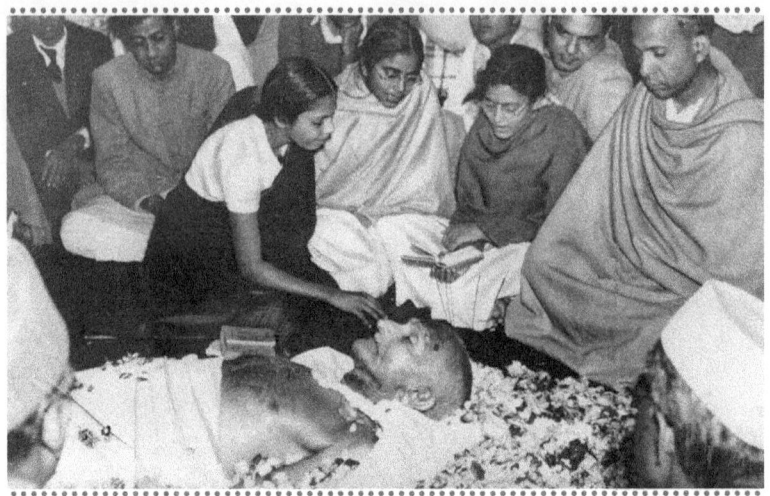

public protests all over the nation for equal rights. In such a scenario, Jawaharlal declared India as a secular nation, as a land belonging to all religions.

After independence, the next step that had to be taken was to form a proper Constitution of India. Jawaharlal Nehru played a vital role in shaping the constitution. It was decided that the nation would be designed as a 'sovereign democratic and republic' state where every citizen irrespective of their caste or creed was to be treated as an equal. It took about two years for the constitution to form and function properly.

On 26 January 1950, the Constitution came into effect. Dr. Rajendra Prasad became the first President of the country. The country was free of monarchy but India agreed to remain as a member of the commonwealth as the British Commonwealth agreed to have a democratic country as its member.

There were still many states in India that were under Princes' rule and did not commit themselves to the Indian Union. Jawaharlal talked to the people of these states. These states were very weak and the princes of the state were not in the position to form their independent states. So, they readily joined the Indian Union in order to survive seclusion.

CHAPTER 16
Issue of Pakistan

Sardar Patel, the Home and the State Minister at that time, had put in a lot of effort in convincing the princes of these provinces. Except for Hyderabad and Kashmir, all states cooperated in the process. But later, when the police forces were enforced in the state, Hyderabad readily agreed to join the Indian Union. But the problems in Kashmir still persisted as raiders from Pakistan demanded the rulers to join Pakistan. But eventually, the rulers refused and joined the Indian Union instead. Stuck in a dilemma, the rulers of Kashmir were the last one to decide whether to join India or Pakistan. Every other ruler whose state fell on the Indian region joined the Indian Union, and the rulers whose state fell under the Pakistan region joined Pakistan, except for Kashmir which fell in the middle.

This wait frustrated the Pakistani rulers. At the end of the year in 1947, the Pakistani rulers organized attackers from the tribal population in the North-West Frontier and sent them across the border into Kashmir. These attackers created a lot of disturbances by ransacking, looting and

killing many innocent people. This shocked the local people as well as the leaders of the country. In a state of panic, the Maharaja left the state by declaring Kashmir as a part of Pakistan.

Jawaharlal Nehru and Sardar Patel decided to defend Kashmir and fight against the attackers. Even though, India does not believe in the use of force, but in order to defend Kashmir, they had to use force. Soon the Indian troops were flown to Kashmir and they successfully defeated the Pakistani attackers. Though Pakistan stated that the attackers were an independent group of terrorists, but in no time their troops were in action. India was capable enough to drive out the Pakistanis completely from Kashmir. But in order to do that they had to attack the Pakistani bases. Such a decision would definitely result in war between the two countries and India did not want that.

But rather than starting a war, in early 1948 India showed great faith in the United Nations and filed a complaint to the Security Council. But the appeal failed to get its due importance and was left unsolved.

Jawaharlal's ancestors were from Kashmir but he had no direct relations with the state. He visited the state to enjoy the beautiful mountains and valleys of Kashmir. The state of Kashmir was beautifully designed to bestow peace, rather than drown itself in bloodshed and killings.

CHAPTER 17
Kashmir

After the death of Jawaharlal Nehru, in September 1965 Pakistan committed a second attack on Kashmir. Firstly, the southern border was attacked and large batches of attackers were sent across the border. They left no other option for India, but to attack. The war was stopped by the Security Council and they asked both the countries to cease-fire. When matters got out of hand, the Soviet Union took the first step by organizing a meet of the Indian and the Pakistani leaders in Tashkent. India agreed and stated their hesitance in using force for settling fights. India insisted on having direct communication with Pakistan in order to settle Kashmir and other disputes. But Pakistan did not accept the meeting to be official and refused to talk directly.

The population of Muslims were a majority in Kashmir. This might have made the leaders across the border think of Kashmir as deserving to be a part of Pakistan. For nearly twenty years, the Muslims of Kashmir have settled down to a life of peace along with the rest of India. The last thing

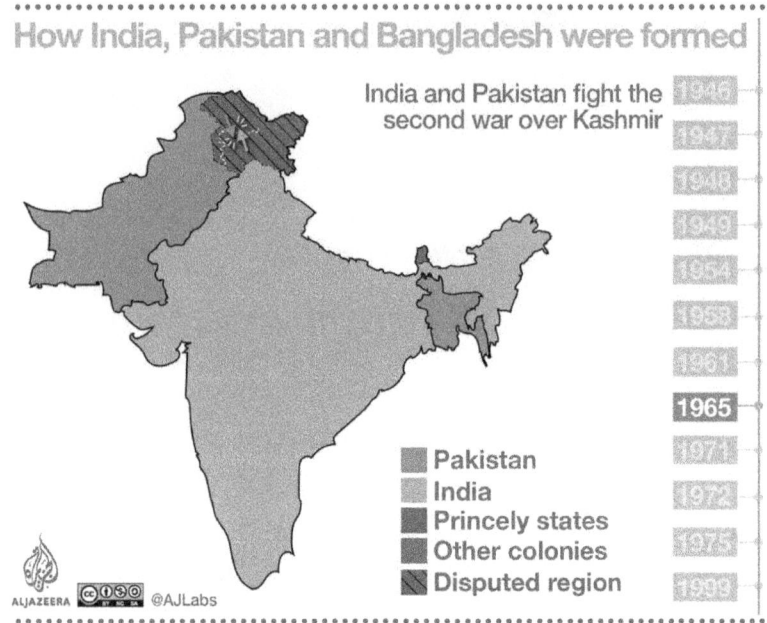

they want is to get disturbed. Timely elections have been held in Kashmir and people have expressed their desire in favour of staying as a part of the Indian Union, while Pakistan have not held direct elections even for its own people. The only time Kashmir gets disturbed, is when Pakistan decides to intrude and use force on the state.

Except for the Kashmir issue, the two nations have no other issues heating up between them. Apart from that, they even share economic relations and India is always the first one to initiate for peace talks.

Jawaharlal was scholarly, clever, and witty. His experience of travelling around the world made him a great scholar in world history. He was well aware about world affairs. He was quite progressive and modern in his thoughts and outlook. He had foreseen and planned the future of the country. He has always imagined India to stand among the developed nations.

He was well known and respected for his achievements in Indian political history. He was not only the head of the cabinet but also the member of external affairs. He had called the Asian Relations Conference which encouraged other Asian nations under colonial rule to fight for their freedom. He had also extended a hand of friendship to the people of Africa.

With the independence of India in 1947, Jawaharlal Nehru took oath as both the Prime Minister and the Foreign Minister. He was capable and determined, and this enabled him to stay as the Foreign Minister till the end of his time. The leaders from all over the world admired him for his knowledge on foreign and external affairs.

CHAPTER 18
The Policy of Non-Alignment

Jawaharlal Nehru was highly influenced by Gandhian beliefs. Therefore, he wanted to introduce truth, non-violence, and apply Gandhian ideology in maintaining the relations between countries. These ideologies sustained the necessary peace that India wanted to keep and emanate. Such an ideology saved a lot of energy and money wasted on developing arms and nuclear weapons like atom bomb and hydrogen bomb. Jawaharlal opposed several military blocs like NATO (the North Atlantic Treaty Organization) and establishment of military bases on unallocated areas. He strongly believed that if all the countries in the world were free from colonial opposition, the world would be a better place to live in.

The dominance and exertion of power of one country over another is called colonialism. Though, India is free from colonial exertion, Jawaharlal Nehru wished other countries be free as well. The effort and approach adopted by India to claim its freedom from the British rule, helped Indonesia and other countries to achieve their independence. He continued extending help to different Asian and African countries till they were all free. For this, Jawaharlal had to face the opposition of various colonial powers like Britain, France, Holland, and other European countries. Their vast range of conquests and possessions were called empires. Even when the old colonies were wiped out, new form of colonialism emerged, for example, when European countries started capturing their former colonies. He also fought against this new form of colonialism.

He had his own set of ideologies. Jawaharlal massively helped India to get its own independence, and also helped other countries to get theirs as well. This characteristic of Nehru was highly praised by people from all over the world. He believed that India's policies were in India's own interests but if other countries were free, it will strengthen India's own freedom. He thought that only when there will

be peace in the world, will there be peace in India as well. He was against the idea of cold war as such wars act as a premonition of a global war to take place. This is why he maintained the neutrality of India by not letting India join either the American bloc or the Soviet bloc. As joining either of the blocs would lead to conflicting situations with the other bloc which would give rise to a clash. India was friendly with both America and the Soviet Union and did not join either of the blocs. This was called the policy of non-alignment. This encouraged other developing countries and the bloc of independent powers to maintain peace.

Both the blocs expected India to join them, but later the idea of non-involvement of India was clear to both America and the Soviet Union. They respected such an arrangement as they felt it helped in maintaining peace by avoiding conflicts between countries. Later, they planned to end the cold war and re-establish friendship between the countries once again!

CHAPTER 19
Supporter of Peace

India acted jointly with other countries to serve peace and was active in the United Nations, where all countries, except for a few, worked together. Jawaharlal supported in establishing peace and did not support the production and use of arms. But in order to establish peace, he did send troops to places where there was trouble. He supported various freedom movements and helped in the development of backward countries.

He also worked to uplift the backward Asian and African countries. In 1954, Jawaharlal attended the Conference of Developing Countries in Bandung in Indonesia. Later, there was a conference of non-aligned countries in Belgrade, in Yugoslavia. Jawaharlal kept travelling to attend such conferences which condemned colonialism, racialism, armaments, and supported peace.

Jawaharlal developed good relations with the President Nasser of Egypt and Marshal Tito of Yugoslavia. They were counted as two of the most respected figures of the non-alignment moment. In 1956, he criticized and

condemned the unwanted bloodshed and violence when Britain, France, and Israel attacked Egypt. He also worked against the notion of atomic warfare. He was also the first one to sign when the treaty against the use of atomic weapons was designed.

Extensive travelling had made him a scholar in foreign affairs. He travelled to many countries to talk about the betterment of the relations of the country with other countries. His works and his achievements left footprints in the minds and hearts of the Government and the people. He developed friendly relations with many countries such as America, the Soviet Union, China, etc. He won several hearts because he stood for peace and cooperation among the nations.

Jawaharlal respected China for the vastness of its population and land. Jawaharlal sympathized with China when it was attacked by Japan before the commencement of the Second World War. He wanted to help China but India at that time, was under the British rule and was not in the condition to extend help. But even though he couldn't help China, he had sent a medical mission on behalf of the Congress as a token of sympathy. When he visited China in September 1939, he saw them defending themselves against Japan. Due to outbreak of war in Europe, he had to return back.

At the time of India's independence, there was an ongoing civil war in China. The Communists, under the leadership of Mao Tse-Tung, were fighting against the Kuomintang, the ruling party. Kuomintang was under the leadership of Chiang Kai-shek. Chiang was dishonest and was thus, hated by the people around him and even lost the support of his own troop members. The Communists swept the Japanese troops out of the country and captured their weapons. As a result of which, Peking, the capital of China, surrendered and the Communists established their rule.

CHAPTER 20
India-China Relationship

Not only did Jawaharlal sympathize with the Chinese revolution, but also was the first to recognize it as a government. Few years after India got its independence; a vast change had taken place in China. China was under a strong and confident government. Jawaharlal earnestly desired India and China to work together as friends, since there never been any past records of conflicts between the two.

There have been many similarities between the two countries. Both had old civilizations which added to the cultural heritage of the country. There had been cultural exchanges between them for many centuries, and they had a common border that ran as long as two thousand miles. India and China were close neighbours and they must maintain the close proximal relation between them. Both Jawaharlal and the Chinese leaders agreed on the fact that it is necessary for peace to be administered between the countries.

In 1950, there was an upsurge in tension between the two countries over Tibet. Tibet had not yet decided on its nationhood and the two countries claimed it to be under their rule. Though it wasn't an independent country, it still was an independent state of China, making China its legal ruler. But irrespective of that, Tibet had a certain amount of freedom. India opposed when China wanted to send troops to Lhasa, the capital of Tibet. Though legally, India had no right over Tibet but in the professional platform, they shared certain trading posts. Losing Tibet, meant loss of those posts too. Jawaharlal stated that as Tibet is a sovereign state, it should be able to enjoy its social and cultural freedom. After much discussion, the Chinese agreed and Dalai Lama was recognized as the ruler of Tibet.

In 1954, both the countries signed a treaty and Tibet regained back its freedom. The principles enclosed in the treaty came to be known as Five Principles of Peace, or Panch-sheel. It was gradually adopted and accepted by most of the countries.

Among countries, India and China share close relations. There had been growth in tourism and cultural connections within both the countries. In 1954, Jawaharlal was received warmly in China. Likewise, Mr. Chou En-lai, the Prime Minister of China received a warm welcome in India more than once. Even the Chinese leaders affirmed that though China and India might have different paths, but there exists a mutual friendship between them. The Chinese were aware of India as an independent country, free of influence of any powerful blocs in the world.

In 1950, a war broke out in Korea. The Chinese supported the people of North Korea who were fighting against the South Koreans. India worked hard to bring

about a cease-fire and Jawaharlal's efforts for peace was highly appreciated by the Chinese. In fact, the Prime Minister of China, Mr. Chou En-lai was helped by India to attend the Bandung Conference.

CHAPTER 21
Differences over the Border

There was peace between China and India, but gradually, the two developed differences over the border. When the treaty on Tibet was signed in 1954, the Chinese did not raise any doubts about the existing border demarcations. The Chinese had illegally captured a large area of India. When Jawaharlal raised the issue in front of the Chinese Prime Minister, he cunningly covered the matter by blaming on the inaccuracy of mapping that was promised to be replaced soon. The issue never surfaced again. The Chinese slowly raised more and more doubts about the border and made occasional thrusts into the Indian Territory.

There was an outbreak of revolt in Lhasa due to suppression of Tibetans by the Chinese government in 1959. This compelled Dalai Lama to take refuge in India so as to save his life. India couldn't refuse to help. When India gave refuge to Dalai Lama, it angered the Chinese government. They started abusing Jawaharlal Nehru and constantly raised disputes over the border. Jawaharlal maintained his calm as he did not want any differences to arise between China and India, for it would run long enough to resolve and would prove as a disadvantage for both the countries.

In 1962, India defended itself against the Chinese advancement to its territory. The Chinese used heavy cavalry and tried to intrude in to the country. Nevertheless, India attacked with same force and power and every individual stood to defend his nation. Jawaharlal knew the condition of India was not strong enough to defend itself as it had just got its independence and was not prepared for a war. He still focused on its development and maintained his calm as he did not want to leave any scope for war.

The Chinese government was well apprised of the strength of India and its people. The Chinese knew they

couldn't advance too far as the Indians were prepared to drive the Chinese back. This stopped the Chinese troops from advancing.

As a leader, Jawaharlal was loved and appreciated by one and all. Everyone admired him for his capabilities as a leader as he intimately knew the people, their interests, and knew how to inspire them. He was known for his competence as a leader, his knowledge, vision for the future, and his belief in democracy. He encouraged the formation of a Constituent Assembly so that people will have the power to choose their own representatives. These representatives will decide how the people would govern themselves. The people were the masters and they themselves will decide their future because democracy is synonymous to freedom.

In democracy, everyone, irrespective of their gender, caste, and creed, would have the right to vote. In order

to increase the literacy rate in India, Jawaharlal Nehru encouraged everyone to learn to read and write. He felt that all adults must choose their own political representatives through elections and people should be taught the feeling of unity. Jawaharlal knew that India was a land of deep-rooted old beliefs. He wanted India to gradually change by itself, without any exercise of force. And most importantly, there shouldn't be any form of division on the basis of religion or caste or languages. There would be no majority or minority culture as all cultures would be regarded as 'Indian'. India would be a country where people live in unity, and not in differences.

CHAPTER 22
Nehru-The Great Follower of Democracy

The sole difference between democracy and autocracy lies in the fact that in democracy, the power is divided among the people and is not concentrated in a few hands. Jawaharlal Nehru was a great democrat and he spoke in a simple and touching way. He was also one of the greatest parliamentarians of the day as he respected the parliament and its decisions. He was a gentleman as he never insulted

his enemies or the people who stood against him. He was a man of principles, highly disciplined, punctual, and not an extremist in emotions.

He was the man of his words, and for him, time was precious. He claimed and believed that democracy had successfully worked in India. Though he played a vital role in regaining back India's independence, he never takes sole credits for his efforts, rather addresses the efforts of the people as a whole.

During its first stage of execution, the people with their sense of facts and expectations were able to choose the right political representative in the four general elections. Even the people who were illiterate took a keen interest in the elections. This made this huge operation a grand success. This was regarded as the largest elections held anywhere in the world. Apart from the urban population, Jawaharlal wanted the people from the rural areas to participate and choose their own political representatives and progress in all fields.

The villagers were encouraged to learn reading and writing. They were also made aware about the modern means of irrigation. The country was trying its best to progress from 'underdeveloped' to 'developed'. Jawaharlal believed that democracy was the only solution for most of the problems. Even when others were in doubt with regard to its future prospects, he had his faith unhindered and that faith was justified.

Owing to the vast geographical and diversified culture, it was a tough job for a leader to take care of all the matters at the same time. Jawaharlal held the office as the Prime Minister for over seventeen years. He was a determined and a diligent worker who worked for hours, till late at night and sometimes till the early hours of the morning. He repeatedly motivated people to work hard to build the country. He sometimes took some time off to relax but never to rest as he strongly believed in his saying:

"Aram haram hai! (To rest is to waste)".

He supported India at its worst and selflessly led it to the path of freedom. Later as the Prime Minister, he made it grow and prosper to create its own unique regime promoting the welfare of its people. He was the heart and soul of the Congress party. In his time period, he represented both the modern and free India. His name was regarded synonymous to India, i.e., Jawaharlal meant India and India meant Jawaharlal. He was passionate in any work he took up, and was both the Prime Minister and the leader of the Congress party. He supplied ideas to the Congress and the Congress lead the government making him an indispensable part of the constitutional framework.

CHAPTER 23
The Man of Strength

As India's Prime Minister, Jawaharlal Nehru arranged meetings with important visitors from abroad and held discussions on different matters with them. He was also a great entertainer. He also visited different countries to strengthen their friendship and maintain peaceful ties with India. He addressed the United Nations once in Paris and twice in New York. There he had called upon the leaders of the world to prefer peace over weaponry. He also spoke to large gatherings of people all over the country and tried to strengthen their patriotic spirit. Under his leadership, many projects started opening in the country and attended functions arranged by them. He tried to intimate himself with the needs and issues of the people which further motivated him to work.

In 1962, Jawaharlal fell ill but he recovered in a few days. He was still regarded as one of the best speakers in the Parliament. He was disappointed when the Chinese attacked India. No matter the kind of situation he had to deal with, he remained calm and never compromised on

his policies. He refused to join the bloc, and the leading countries of both the blocs supported India.

As a leader, he was highly ambitious, able and knew the people of the nation very well. He was proud of his country and its people and also of their capacity and courage to survive the worst. Even during his illness, all he wanted was to keep working for his country. As stated by him, his last ambition was to dedicate the rest of his days to the development of the nation. He wanted to do his best before his death. He never cared about opinions and he was satisfied in his job, works and achievements.

He was always regarded as a man of strength for the nation and its people. When finally his body didn't allow him to work, he decided to resign from the post of the Prime Minister at the age of seventy. He had tried resigning two times earlier but couldn't proceed because of the love of the people and his passion to make India shine at its best. He felt equally responsible when he left his office; he personally dealt with the problems of India and continued working with the same perseverance even after his first illness in 1962.

CHAPTER 24
End of the Great Soul

Even in his old days, he was equally energetic and passionate. He continued to work despite his poor health. In January 1963, during a session of the All India Congress in Bhubaneswar, Odisha, he experienced a mild stroke. His left side was partially paralyzed. But still he didn't stop and, continued with his work. He returned to Delhi immediately to take some rest but he could not. He had to fly to the India-Nepal Border to oversee the progress of an irrigation plant.

He regularly attended the Parliamentary proceedings and worked for the planning commission. He shocked everyone with his speeches when he came to attend the meeting of the All India Congress Committee in Bombay. He also participated in the events organized by the Committee.

In May 1964, he was forced by the doctors and his family to take adequate rest. Therefore he decided to fly to Dehradun and spend his time in writing. He was happy to meet his old friends and family after so long. The trip refreshed him back to work. He returned back to Delhi on May 26th. He earnestly worked till midnight and woke up the next day feeling a bit uncomfortable. He even informed his assistant about his ill-health. He lay down on his bed and was unable to get up. Doctors were called who tried in their best possible way to make him feel comfortable.

His life and health was indispensable for the people and the nation. Indira was worried and was sitting beside him. The news of his ill-health rapidly spread across the country. Everyone was shocked and was praying for his good-health. The people were so used to his presence that his absence seemed devastating.

But on 27th May, at 2 p.m., he lost his struggle with death and was declared dead. The whole country was mourning at the news of his death. The noblest leader of all times was no more. The news of his death created a vacuum in the hearts of all Indians. The whole world was shocked to hear the news. The ongoing parliamentary session was cancelled. Leaders from all over the world sent condolences and the atmosphere of death shrouded the whole country.

Jawaharlal was cremated on the morning of May 28th with due honours from the State as a token of respect. Many governmental representatives from remote countries had arrived to attend the funeral.

Shantivan is a place at Raj Ghat, New Delhi, where the Samadhi of the great leader Jawaharlal Nehru is built as a symbol for commemorating the great figure. Presently, it is regarded as a place of pilgrimage.

Great words of Jawaharlal Nehru:

All other dreams disappear and are reduced to ashes without peace.

The art of a people is the true mirror of their mind.

Peace is not a relationship of nations but it is a condition of mind brought about by a serenity of soul.

"Aaram Haaram Haram: To Rest is to Waste."

www.ingramcontent.com/pod-product-compliance
Lightning Source LLC
LaVergne TN
LVHW091317080426
835510LV00007B/524